HISTORIC ALBANY

City & County

by Bill Buell

A publication of the Albany County Historical Association

Historical Publishing Network
A division of Lammert Incorporated
San Antonio, Texas

CONTENTS

3 CHAPTER I   *An Introduction*

11 CHAPTER II   *Early Albany*

16 CHAPTER III   *Bethlehem*

20 CHAPTER IV   *Colonie*

24 CHAPTER V   *Guilderland*

29 CHAPTER VI   *New Scotland & Coeymans*

33 CHAPTER VII   *Albany's Hilltowns*

35 SPECIAL THANKS

36 SHARING THE HERITAGE

First Edition

Copyright © 2012 Historical Publishing Network

ISBN: 9781935377887

Library of Congress Card Catalog Number: 2012943784

Historic Albany: City and County

author:	Bill Buell
cover artist:	John Hart
contributing writer for sharing the heritage:	Garnette Bane

Historical Publishing Network

president:	Ron Lammert
project managers:	Violet Caren
	Bob Sadoski
	Larry Sunderland
	James Williams
administration:	Donna M. Mata
	Melissa G. Quinn
book sales:	Dee Steidle
production:	Colin Hart
	Evelyn Hart
	Glenda Tarazon Krouse
	Omar Wright
	Tony Quinn
	Tim Lippard

Fort Orange, Rensselaerswijck
Albany, New York, circa 1650
L.F. Tantillo 2009

CHAPTER I

AN INTRODUCTION

Around 3 p.m. on the afternoon of October 9, 1777, about eighteen hundred men from Albany County charged over the crest of a hill in a farmer's wheat field near Bemis Heights in what is today the town of Stillwater. You could almost hear a collective gasp from the British troops facing them. Gentleman Johnny Burgoyne's Saratoga Campaign was ending badly. He would not reach Albany and occupy it, and his goal of assuming power in New York and dividing the colonies would fail. The tide of the American Revolution had changed, and with it so too the course of world history.

It was Abraham Ten Broeck who led those Albany men into battle that day, a confrontation that makes many top ten lists of the most significant military engagements in world history. Born in 1734 of hearty Dutch stock, Ten Broeck was one of the leading figures in Colonial Albany, twice serving as mayor after having been chairman of the New York Provincial Congress and a delegate to the Second Continental Congress.

There were a handful of prominent men in Albany during Ten Broeck's day, and most of them represented New York's aristocratic ruling class. To many, the decision to remain a subject of the King and maintain the status quo, or risk life and liberty and help mankind usher in a new form of freedom, wasn't an easy one. The Van Rensselaers, the Livingstons and the Schuylers were all a bit hesitant to play their hand too early in the debate between the colonies and the mother country, but Ten Broeck, it seems, was an avid and early believer in the patriot cause.

When Ten Broeck led the militia into battle at Saratoga that day, they were defending their home. The land they were fighting on was part of Albany County. When it was formed in 1683 as one of New York's twelve original counties, Albany's boundaries were vast and vague, encompassing much of upstate New York as well as most of what is now Vermont. And, to some haughty local officials, the county line to the west extended as far as the Pacific Ocean.

As the peopling of New York continued and the necessity for more accessible local government became apparent, Albany County was divided into smaller units. It was the creation of two new counties from what is now Vermont—Cumberland County in 1766 and Gloucester County in 1770 —that first significantly reduced the size of Albany County. Then, in March of 1772, the colonial legislature continued to change Albany's borders and decrease its power, adding Tryon County to the west and Charlotte County to the north.

In this painting, Fort Orange and the Patroon's House, *artist Len Tantillo gives us a good idea of what Fort Orange looked like sometime between 1624-1664. The fort was surrounded by a stone-lined moat on all four sides, and access to the interior was gained by a small bridge at the main gate that faced the river. The Patroon's House is to the right, outside the fort, and wasn't actually occupied by a Van Rennselaer until Kiliaen's grandson, Jan Baptiste, came to America and moved into the home sometime after 1652.*

Above: The Albany Congress was held from June 19-July 11 in 1754 with seven different colonies sending representatives. Many of the most prominent men of the day were in attendance, including Benjamin Franklin, William Johnson and Thomas Hutchinson. In this image, Mohawk sachem Hendrick talks to Franklin and other Colonial leaders inside Albany's City Hall.

Below: Spelling wasn't a priority for the 17th century Dutch as this early map of Albany County and the location of the "Mannor of Renslaer" and the "Mannor of Livingston" clearly indicate.

However, as the American Revolution descended upon New York, Albany County remained considerably larger than it is today. And, as the war drew to a close, it still included the area now claimed by Columbia, Rensselaer, Saratoga and Schenectady counties, as well as large parts of Greene and Washington counties and, according to Albany officials, a section of southwestern Vermont. But the post-Revolution era resulted in even more changes. In 1786 the creation of Columbia County altered the political landscape, as did the formation of Rensselaer and Washington counties in 1791, Schoharie County in 1795 and Greene County in 1800. Finally, when Schenectady County was mapped out in 1809, Albany County's geographical boundaries became basically what they are today.

The county seat is Albany, which also serves as the capital city of New York. It was originally called Fort Orange when the Dutch began settling the area in the early 17th century, about 15 years after Henry Hudson sailed up what he called the North River in 1609 looking for the Northwest Passage. He only got as far as present-day Albany, and while Hudson didn't find an easy way to the Orient, he did discover that the fur trade would prove to be a very profitable business in the New World.

In 1624 about twenty families of French Walloons and Protestant refugees under the auspices of the Dutch West India Company sailed up the Hudson and built Fort Orange, named after Maurice, the Prince of Orange. By 1629 the company's hierarchy decided that New Netherland was a losing proposition, and composed a new way of colonization called patroonships. Kiliaen Van Rensselaer's was by far the most successful and enduring of these feudal-like arrangements, his property encompassing seven hundred thousand acres and portions of present-day Albany, Rensselaer, Columbia and Greene Counties.

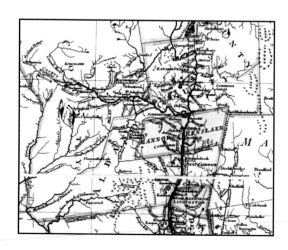

It was nearly the same type of environment many of the new arrivals in New Netherland had left in Europe, and as more and more people came across the Atlantic, Van Rensselaer's colonial estate—it was called the Manor of Rensselaerwyck—continued to grow. The colony was soon on sound footing, but Father Isaac Jogues, a French missionary who the Dutch had earlier saved from the Mohawks, was not impressed. In 1642 he wrote that Fort Orange was a "miserable" place, and that the "colony is composed of about a hundred persons, who reside in some 25 or 30 houses… solely of boards and thatched, with no mason-work except the chimneys."

While relations between the colonists and the nearby native Americans—most of them were Mahicans—were usually quite tranquil, tensions did rise between the proprietors of Rensselaerwyck and the governing body of the nearby village that was also increasing in size. In 1652, Peter Stuyvesant, the governor of New Netherland, proclaimed that Fort Orange would be called Beverwyck and was to be disassociated from Rensselaerwyck.

The town took on the name of Albany when the English took over control of New Netherland in 1664, and in 1686 it was chartered as a city by Thomas Dongan, the royal governor. Pieter Schuyler, one of Albany's leading citizens, was appointed its first mayor. He was such a popular leader that when troops from New York City approached Albany in 1689 with the goal of assuming command and appointing new leaders—all this as a result of the Glorious Revolution—Schuyler refused. Backed by the entire community as well as all the native Americans in the vicinity, Schuyler retained control of Albany, and Jacob Leisler's three sloops filled with soldiers turned around and headed meekly back down the Hudson River.

At times in the 17th and 18th centuries there were deadly incursions by the Indians, mostly with the aid and encouragement of their French allies. During the American Revolution it was the British who instigated a number of Indian attacks, all of them in the outlying regions of the county. The most memorable and deadly incident occurred in 1781 near the village of Berne when William Dietz and his family were attacked and killed.

Although both Philip Schuyler and Ten Broeck were the objects of unsuccessful kidnapping attempts by Tories and their Indian accomplices during the Revolution, the city of Albany remained a relatively safe place to be throughout the 18th century. In 1754 it hosted the Albany Congress, an attempt by the colonies to help ensure their "mutual defense and security," with the hope of "expanding the British dominance in North America." Leaders such as Benjamin Franklin attended the meeting, but only seven of the original 13 colonies sent delegates and even those failed to ratify what was called "Albany's Plan of Union."

While many of Albany County's citizens had moved closer to the safety of the city during the Revolution, the Treaty of 1783 meant that many people would be returning to their farms, joined by an influx of new settlers looking for their own land, many of them soldiers who had fought during the war. In 1788 a fledgling New York State government divided Rensselaerwyck into two towns—Watervliet on the west side of the Hudson and Beverwyck on the east. Watervliet, now a city on the western banks of the Hudson, encompassed much of present-day Albany County and extended to the northwest well into what is today the Town of Niskayuna in Schenectady County.

Often referred to as the "Mother of Towns," Watervliet spawned 10 new townships, beginning in 1790 with Rensselaerville and then Coeymans in 1791. They were followed by Bethlehem in 1793, Berne in 1795, Guilderland in 1803, Westerlo in 1815, Knox in 1822, New Scotland in 1832, Colonie in 1895, and Green Island in 1896.

Each of those towns has its own distinct and fascinating history, and within their boundaries are authentically American villages such as

This sketch of Native Americans in their canoe greeting Henry Hudson and his ship, the Halfmoon, was done in 1909 by S. Hollyer to help commemorate the event's bicentennial year.

Altamont, Menands, Slingerlands and Voorheesville. Much of the county, in particular the Albany hilltowns, was heavily involved in the Anti-Rent Wars of the 1840s, while the city of Albany remained a transportation hub throughout the 19th century, playing a key role in the building of the Erie Canal and the Mohawk-Hudson Railroad.

Politically, Albany elected its first Irish Catholic mayor, Michael Nolan, in 1878, six years before Boston did the same, and iconic figures like Erastus Corning, Erastus Corning II and Dan O'Connell helped keep the Democrats in control throughout the city and much of the county.

It was Republican Governor Nelson Rockefeller, however, who oversaw the bulding of the Empire State Plaza in the 1960s, giving downtown Albany its look today. Cohoes and Watervliet, the county's two other cities, nestle up to the Hudson River just north of Albany, while the rest of the county is a diverse mix of suburbia, farmland, and forests. Along with the river that serves as its eastern boundary, the county's two major natural landmarks, the Cohoes Falls and the Helderbergs, seem as unchanged as when they were first seen by the Dutch four hundred years ago.

Left: Benjamin Franklin proposed the Albany Plan of Union at the Albany Congress in 1754.

Below: The five photographs of Albany making up this panoramic image were taken sometime before 1906. The dominant building, just left of center, is Albany City Hall, while also visible is the original Livingston Avenue railroad bridge heading over the Hudson River. In the first frame is the old Albany Academy building, while the domed structure just to the left of City Hall is the State New York Court of Appeals. In the third frame are St. Peter's Church and the old Albany Post Office, while to the extreme right is the Cathedral of the Immaculate Conception.

View of Bryans Place   by Hooker.

❖

Above: Philip Schuyler came from a prominent Albany family and married into another one, the Van Rensselaers. Schuyler was born in 1733, married Catherine in 1755, and was a captain during the French and Indian War. During the American Revolution he was the General of the Colonial army's Northern Department before being relieved of duty in 1777 and replaced by Horatio Gates. Schuyler died in 1804, just two days shy of his 71st birthday and four months following the death of his son-in-law, Alexander Hamilton, in his famous duel with Aaron Burr.

Top, right: The Schuyler Mansion was built in 1761-62 as the new home for Philip Schuyler and his wife Catherine Van Rensselaer. The brick mansion located at 32 Catherine St. in Albany is now a state historic site and a museum. It was declared a National Historic Landmark in 1967.

Bottom, right: DeWitt Clinton was the sixth governor of New York and the man largely responsible for the building of the Erie Canal and the formation of the Mohawk-Hudson Railroad. He grew up in Little Britain in Orange County, the son of American Revolutionary War general James Clinton. Also a U.S. senator and vice-president, Clinton died in Albany during his fourth term as governor in 1828.

Left: This image from around 1900 shows a trolley car pulling up to the intersection at State Street and Broadway in downtown Albany.

Bottom, left: This image, from an Albany newspaper in 1921, refers to the ten-month long strike by employees of the United Traction Company. One of the longest mass transit strikes in history, the work stoppage was brought about when company officials refused to negotiate with leaders of the union, members of the Amalgamated Association of Streetcar Workers. Many Albanians, sympathetic to the strikers, refused to ride in the few cars that were being used during the strike.

Below: The Ten Broeck Mansion, home to Abraham Ten Broeck, was built in 1797 and placed on the National Register of Historic Places in 1971. The home was originally called "Prospect," and then changed to "Arbor Hill" when the Olcott family purchased it 1848. It has been home to the Albany County Historical Association since 1948.

Boo Hoo! Boo Hoo! They Won't Ride In My Cars!

❖

Right: This image, taken sometime around 1920, shows the Albany City Savings Bank, the city's first skyscraper. Marcus Reynolds, the famous architect who designed the D&H building, also designed the bank

Bottom, left: A present-day map of Albany County showing its ten towns and other municipalities.

Bottom, right: Albany's City Hall was designed by Henry Hobson Robinson and completed in 1883. The Carillon Tower, which was added on in 1927, reaches 202 feet into the air. The building was added to the National Register of Historic Places in 1972.

CHAPTER II

EARLY ALBANY

❖

Above: The Cohoes Falls is the second largest falls east of the Mississippi River in terms of cubic feet per second, surpassed only by Niagara Falls. It was first seen by Europeans in the early seventeenth century, and soon became a major tourist attraction. The falls, between 75 and 90 feet high and 1,000 feet wide, occurs just before the Mohawk River concludes it's 500-mile west to east route from its source in the Tughill Plateau in central New York. A few hundred yards after the falls, the Mohawk breaks up into three main tributaries and flows into the Hudson River.

Below: Harmony Mills became the largest manufacturer of cotton in the world during the second half of the 19th century. This view, looking to the southeast, shows the enlarged Erie Canal in the foreground as well as Harmony Mill Building No. 3 on the left and Harmony Mill Building No. 1 on the right.

Clockwise from top, left:

A section of the original 1825 Erie Canal, in the foreground, was used by Harmony Mill No. 3, the centerpiece building of the complex which opened in 1872.

Horace Silliman built the Silliman Memorial Church at the corner of Mohawk and Ontario Streets as a gift to the city in 1896. Although the building was on the National Register of Historic Places, it was demolished in 1998.

The old Cohoes Opera House on Remsen Street early in the twentieth century was a popular place to be. Built in the 1890s, it was surrounded by the Cohoes Hotel on the left and the Masonic Temple on the right. The building was demolished in 2010.

These buildings along Ontario Street in Cohoes were built just before the turn of the twentieth century. At the near right is City Hall, designed by J. C. Holland and built in 1895, and adjacent to it is the Silliman Memorial Church, built in 1896 as a gift to the city by Horace Silliman, a Cohoes native and 1846 Union College graduate. Further down the street is the Moose Club. The district was added to the National Register of Historic Places in 1979.

On August 5, 1919, Henry Ford carved his initials into what would become the cornerstone of the new Ford Motor Company plant in Green Island. Also pictured with Ford are Thomas Edison on the left, holding his cap, Harvey Firestone, behind Ford, and John Burroughs (bearded). Also in the photo are Albany mayor James R. Watt, to the right of Edison, and Troy mayor Cornelius Burns, between Firestone and Burroughs.

Left: These Green Island factory buildings were used by the Rensselaer and Saratoga Railroad and the Delaware and Hudson Railroad. The building, now demolished, was on Tibbits Avenue in Green Island.

Below: Two trolley cars make their way to the intersection of Broadway and 16th St. in Watervliet, in this image from circa 1900. The Collins House is on the right.

Cor. Broadway & 16th St. Watervliet N.Y.

Top: On March 28, 1913, the Hudson River flooded into Watervliet as far as 2nd Street and was measured up to depths of eight feet along Broadway.

Middle: The gun shop foreman and his mechanics at the Watervliet Arsenal posed for this photograph in 1901 with a 16' breech loading rifle in front of the north wing of the Seacoast gun shop.

Bottom: The San Souci Theatre on 16th St. was a popular movie house in Watervliet around the turn of the twentieth century.

❖

Left: The Meneely Bell Company manufactured over sixty-five thousand bells from 1826 until it closed in 1952. The original shop, shown here in 1913, was built by Andrew Meneely in Watervliet. A third son opened another factory in Troy.

❖

Top: Two busses from the Slingerlands, Delmar, Elsmere and Albany line are parked outside Hungerford Garage on Kenwood Avenue in 1925.

Middle: The Bethlehem Historical Association moved into the Cedar Hill Schoolhouse at 1003 River Road in Selkirk in 1965. It had been built in 1859 and redesigned into its present configuration in 1907 by Albany architect Marcus Reynolds.

Bottom: The Adams House Hotel still stands and was once a popular place in Delmar. Built in 1836 by Nathaniel Adams, it was a hotel and also a post office before becoming the Bethlehem Town Hall from 1950-80.

1917

❖

Top: Cornelius H. Slingerland opened the Slingerland Printing Company in 1879. It was purchased by the Burland Company in 1940 and was closed down in 1946. It is located on New Scotland Avenue right by the railroad overpass.

Middle: John Martin opened his blacksmith shop in 1886 on the northeast corner of Glenmont Road and Route 9W in the hamlet of Bethlehem Center, now known as Glenmont.

Bottom: Delaware Avenue was still a dirt road when this photograph was taken at the turn of the century. The view is looking to the East, and the sign on the store to the left indicates that gasoline was for sale.

Top: Some of Delmar's most prominent citizens were joined by a marching band and some young boys during this Fourth of July parade, c. 1920.

Middle, left: The Slingerlands Tollgate was on New Scotland Avenue, near the Slingerland Printing Company, on the left. This view is to the East, and the road heading off to the right is Kenwood Avenue.

Middle, right: The Kenwood Tollgate was located on South Pearl Street in what was then called Kenwood (in the town of Bethlehem) and is now the city of Albany. The tollgate monitored traffic on the Albany and Bethlehem Turnpike.

Bottom: The Slingerlands Village Wonders was a popular baseball team between 1901-1915. Playing teams from all over Albany and Schoharie County, the Wonders' home games were at a field just north of today's Cherry Arms Apartments on the west side of Cherry Avenue. They also played near the intersection of Kenwood and Union Avenue and on Mullens Road in Slingerlands.

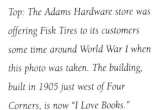

Top: The Adams Hardware store was offering Fisk Tires to its customers some time around World War I when this photo was taken. The building, built in 1905 just west of Four Corners, is now "I Love Books."

Middle: The Delmar Fire Engine Company No. 1 posed for this photograph sometime before the turn of the century. The image is from a postcard.

Bottom: Students posing for a photograph in front of the Cedar Hill School, now home to the Bethlehem Historical Association in Selkirk.

Below: This house at 1511 New Scotland Avenue in Slingerlands was used in the 1987 film Ironweed, starring Jack Nicholson and Meryl Streep. It was built in 1876 for Charles D. Hammond, superintendent of the Delaware & Hudson Railroad. The movie was based on William Kennedy's 1984 Pulitzer Prize-winning novel..

CHAPTER IV

COLONIE

❖

Right: The Albany Car Wheel Company was located in the village of Menands on the eastern side of Rt. 32 or Broadway, near the old Montgomery Ward Building. This photo, c. 1910, shows the very first section of the Erie Canal.

Below: Brewster & Sons Carriage Manufacturers, seen here circa 1900, was at the intersection of Maxwell Road and Route 9 in Newtonville. The building was totally destroyed by fire.

❖

Above: The miniature railroad ride was one of the most popular things to do at Al-Tro Island Park, built in 1907 in Menands along the Hudson River not too far from the Albany city line. The park, which took its name from Albany and Troy, opened in 1907.

Bottom, left: Alton (also called Alta) McDonald was a popular driver and trainer of harness horses. Born in 1854 in Hartford, McDonald died in 1911 and is buried at Vale Cemetery. Among the popular horses he raced to victories were Prince Albert, Major Delmar and Sweet Marie.

Bottom, right: Panetta's Restaurant, formerly McDonald's Hotel, operated from August of 1948 through February of 1959 before it was demolished to make way for the new highway. The hotel was built sometime before 1891.

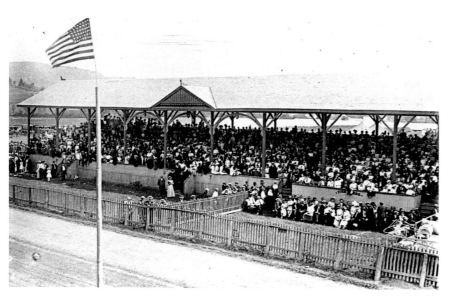

Top, left: A large crowd fills the grandstand at Al-Tro Island Park to watch a horse race. The park formally opened on Memorial Day in 1907 and consisted of a boardwalk 900 feet long and 40 feet wide with amusements along each side. It closed sometime in the 1920s.

Top, right: This Beers map of 1891 shows the Menands area.

Middle: This Albany Senators team photo from the early 1940s shows player-manager Rip Collins in the middle of the front row with batboy Jimmy McCaffrey on his lap. A major league star at one time with the St. Louis Cardinals' Gashouse Gang, Collins acted as player-manager with the Senators from 1942-46. McCaffrey was the son of team owner Thomas McCaffrey.

Bottom: A military band played music before an Albany Senators' game in the 1940s. The Senators were one of the first professional baseball teams to play a night game under the lights.

❖

Above: Babe Ruth came to Hawkins Stadium on April 22, 1935, to play an exhibition game as a member of the Boston Braves. The Braves defeated the Albany Senators, 10-4, before 4,000 fans, and 8-year-old Jimmy McDonald of Menands got to spend a few minutes with the Babe and had his picture taken by a Times-Union photographer.

Top, left: New York Governor Nelson Rockefeller and Albany Senators' team owner Thomas McCaffrey talk about the upcoming 1959 season in Albany, which would be the Senators last.

Middle: Josiah Stanford and his wife Elizabeth moved to Roessleville in the Town of Colonie in 1840 and ran this tavern called the Elm Grove Hotel. Their son Leland, born in 1834, became the governor of California along with forming Stanford University.

Bottom: This Shaker meeting house, on the grounds of the Shaker Heritage Society in the Town of Colonie, was built in 1848. A religious sect which believed in celibacy, the Shakers were formed at that location in 1776 by Ann Lee, who had emigrated from England two years earlier.

CHAPTER V

GUILDERLAND

❖

Right: The Mynderse-Frederick House was built by Nicholas Mynderse in 1802 on what was then called the Schoharie Turnpike and what is now Route 146 in Guilderland Center. Mynderse, Guilderland's first town supervisor, sold the building in 1820 to Michael Frederick whose family ran it as a tavern until 1917 when they turned it into their family home. In this 1890 photo, William Frederick poses for the camera while his son, William Jr., handles the horses. The building is now home to the Guilderland Historical Society.

Below: The Will Mynderse Farm was located across Route 146 from the Mynderse-Frederick House. In this c. 1890 photo, John Wormer is in charge of the horses, while from left are Mabel Tullock, her mother Mrs. Tullock, Mrs. Shannon, and Andrew Tullock.

❖

Top, left: This photo, taken around 1900, shows the Guilderland Iosco baseball team playing a game against another team. Iosco was the name of the store at the corner of Foundry and Western Turnpike owned by the family of Henry Rowe Schoolcraft, a Guilderland native and prominent American geographer and ethnologist known for his studies of native American cultures.

Top, right: The Albany and Guilderland Center Bus Line drove its passengers as far as Altamont. This photo, from 1913, was taken on Western Avenue near the old Albany Country Club.

Middle: This house was built by Billy McKown around 1800 at the corner of Fuller Road and Western Turnpike, and used as a tavern for much of the 19th century. McKown, a Guilderland town supervisor from 1813 to 1824, sold the place to William Witbeck in 1884, and the building was destroyed by fire in 1917.

Bottom: McKown's Grove, opened in 1896, became a popular picnic and swimming spot for Albanians trying to get out of the city heat for nearly a century, closing in 1980. It was run by William "Squire" McKown, the grandson of Billy McKown, who owned the original tavern on the corner of Fuller Road and Route 20. This photograph was taken around 1960..

Top: This crossing of the West Shore Railroad was on Wagner Road and was replaced by the Route 146 overpass in 1927.

Middle: Mrs. Williams, the tollkeeper's wife, and two unidentified men posed for this photo sometime late in the 19th century. A milk cart in the background prepares to go through the tollgate, which was located in Westmere where the Turnpike Drive-In was located

Bottom: The Redmen's Hall or Wigwam was located on the south side of Western Turnpike just east of Willow Street. The building was originally a Baptist church, and the group was originally a fraternity founded in 1765 and may have been Guilderland's Sons of Liberty organization. The building was also used by a temperance group, and was also a Catholic Church, a polling place and a Red Cross station.

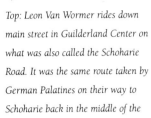

Top: Leon Van Wormer rides down main street in Guilderland Center on what was also called the Schoharie Road. It was the same route taken by German Palatines on their way to Schoharie back in the middle of the eighteenth century.

Middle: Altamont, incorporated as a village in 1890, had its first railroad station built in 1887 by the Delaware and Hudson Railroad. The Albany & Susquehanna Railroad ran through Altamont for the first time in 1867, and the last passenger train passed through on January 23, 1964. The building is now the Altamont Free Library.

Bottom: Charles Brust opened a blacksmith shop and wagon factory sometime around 1880 on Main Street in Guilderland Center. In this photo, circa 1905, Brust stands next to a carriage while his son, Horace, also poses for the camera.

Top: The Chappel family of Parkers Corners posed for this photograph sometime around 1910. Parkers Corners was the area where Route 158 and Old State Road intersect.

Middle: An eastbound passenger train rolls along the West Shore Railroad trestle at French's Hollow sometime in 1898. The last passenger train to use the trestle was in 1959.

Bottom: Abel French built this woolen mill around 1800. Peter Broeck was the first major businessman in the French's Hollow area, building a clothing factory and grist mill using the water power from the nearby Normanskill back in 1795. The industries flourished for a little over 50 years, and the building in this photo was demolished in 1917. The photograph was taken around 1890.

CHAPTER VI

NEW SCOTLAND & COEYMANS

Left: J. M. Erwin, most likely second from the right, stands outside his general store in New Salem with three other men sometime around 1902. Erwin started the business in 1875, but had to rebuild in 1899 after a fire destroyed his first building. More recently, the building was home to Mac's Superette from 1950-72, and it is now being used as an apartment building.

Below: D.C. Gould stands outside his confectionary store in Clarksville around 1890. Gould, who also repaired clocks and watches, lost his business in 1912 when a fire destroyed his building as well as the Central Hotel and its carriage shed just to the right.

❖

Above: Middleburgh native Bouck White posed for this shot in 1912 when he was working for the Holy Trinity Episcopal Church in Brooklyn. An author, minister and artist, Bouck was referred to by Socialist leader Eugene Debs as, "the only Christian minister" in New York. After a failed marriage, White moved to New Scotland in the 1930s and built his home called Federalberg.

Top, right: Federalberg, the home to Socialist minister Bouck White, was built in the Helderbergs in 1934 and was partially destroyed by a fire in 1944. It was still being used as a home throughout the first decade of the 21st century.

Middle: David Haswell Wayne, left, and an employee stand next to his Chevrolet truck outside his blue coal business in Voorheesville around 1928. Through the alleyway the Duffy-Mott Cider Mill can be seen in the distance.

Bottom: Two travelers take a break from their horse and buggy ride on the old Indian Ladder Road along the Helderberg Escarpment around 1900. Today, visitors to the John Boyd Thacher Park take stairs leading to the old Indian trail.

❖

Top, left: Magdalena LaGrange Merritt, a poet and author of "Helderberg Harmonies" and "Songs of the Helderbergs," was a young girl when she posed for this photo circa 1880. Magdalena was one of 16 children born to Myndert and Julia LaGrange.

Top, right: New Salem is a small hamlet in the Town of New Scotland located along the Helderberg Escarpment. This image, from around 1940, is at the bottom of the hill where Route 85A comes in from the west and rejoins Route 85.

Below: This postcard from circa 1900 shows the Empire Cider and Vinegar Works in Voorheesville. The business began in 1890 and in 1917 was sold to Duffy Mott who continued operations until 1956.

❖

Clockwise from top:

In 1894, Magdalena LaGrange married Aaron Merritt of Voorheesville and the couple lived in this house that belonged to her parents on LaGrange Lane just off Ostrander Road.

The hamlet of Coeymans within the Town of Coeymans was a popular place at the turn of the 20th century. In this image, circa 1900-1905, a steamship stops at the Coeymans Dock on the Hudson River. It was one of many that stopped daily at the Coeymans Dock.

This structure, built in 1858, was originally the short-lived Coeymans Academy and then became Coeymans High School.

Coeymans is named after Barent Pieterse Coeymans, who first showed up in the area in 1636 to work for the Van Rensselaer family. This image of the hamlet of Coeymans, circa 1900, is looking north on Main Street along today's Route 144.

CHAPTER VII

ALBANY'S HILLTOWNS

Top, left: The Preston Hollow Methodist Episcopal Church was organized in 1840, and this church was built in 1845 and then remodeled in 1884, adding a tower.

Top, middle: The Berne Hotel, built in 1824 by Daniel Simmons and shown here sometime late in the nineteenth century, is now home to the Berne Town Hall, the Berne Public Library and the Berne Historical Society. Owned by Will Reinhart during the 1850s, it was one of three hotels in Berne during that time.

Top, right: Stephen Van Rensselaer was born in 1764 and lived until 1839. Along with serving as a member of the U.S. House of Representatives and being responsible for the formation of the Mohawk-Hudson Railroad and Rensselaer Polytechnic Institute, he was a descendent of the original patroon, Kiliaen Van Rensselaer. While he was described as a "lenient and benevolent landlord," upon his death his two sons, Stephen and William, began in earnest to collect back debts owed the family and the Anti-Rent War were underway, lasting until 1846 when the state constitution was changed, outlawing the patroon system.

Bottom, left: Just prior to summer vacation in 1932, the last class of the East Berne School District posed for this photograph. Charles Scrafford was the teacher, and the photo was provided to the Berne Historical Society by Bob Goetz, the fourth boy in from the left.

Bottom, middle: This postcard from around the turn of the twentieth century shows Thompson's Lake as seen from the Hotel Piazza. The lake was a popular swimming spot and summer retreat for many Albanians during the late 19th and early 20th century.

Bottom, right: Abundant water power made Rensselaerville a popular place for 18th century settlement, and the first grist mill was built by Samuel Jenkins in 1789 at this location. It is now home to the Rensselaerville Historical Society's Museum.

Top, left: Chester Warner was born in 1885 on the family farm at Warner's Lake. He moved to New Scotland and worked as a carpenter before moving back to Warner's Lake where he married Camille Gallup on June 23, 1927. He died in Schenectady in 1965.

Top, middle: Homer Gallup, a farmer, teacher and mailman, poses with his daughter Camille in his brand new 1915 Ford, one of the first to show up in East Berne.

Top, right: This sign in the hamlet of Rensselaerville gives one the indication that at one time Rensselaerville was the center of New York State and perhaps even North America.

Bottom, left: Wallace E. Deitz, a doctor in the hamlet of Berne, enjoyed showing off his brand new 1906 Ford with his third wife, Theodora, and their two dogs. Deitz was born in 1856 and died in 1928.

Bottom, right: Lt. Michael H. Barckley was born in Knox in 1840 and graduated from Union College before joining the Union army during the Civil War. A lietunent in the Seventh New York Heavy Artillery, Barckley was wounded at the Battle of Cold Harbor and died later in a Washington, D.C., Hospital. The Altamont chapter of the Grand Army of the Republic was named in his honor.

SPECIAL THANKS

These individuals and groups helped greatly with the production of this book.

Tony Opalka, City of Albany Historian, 21 McKinley St., Albany, N.Y. 12206.

Alice Begley, Town of Guilderland Historian, Guilderland Town Hall, P.O. Box 339, Guilderland, N.Y. 12084.

Guilderland Historical Society (Mary Ellen Johnson), 46 Hiawatha Drive, Guilderland, N.Y. 12084.

Kevin Franklin, Town of Colonie Historian, Memorial Town Hall, Newtonville, N.Y. 12128.

Susan Leath, Town of Bethlehem Historian, Bethlehem Town Hall, Delmar, N.Y. 12054.

Spindle City Historic Society (Daniele Cherniak), P.O. Box 375, Cohoes, N.Y. 12047.

Harold (Hal) Miller (albanyhilltowns.com).

Town of Berne Historical Society, Berne New York.

Berne Historical Center, Main St., P.O. Box 34, Berne, N.Y. 12023

Town of Berne Historian, Ralph Miller.

Town of New Scotland Historical Association (Alan Kowlowitz), P.O. Box 541, Voorheesville, N.Y. 12186.

Watervliet Historical Society (Tom Ragostsa) 1501 1st St., Watervliet, N.Y. 12189.

Town of Coeymans Historian Harry Sturges.

Town of Rensselaerville Historical Society, P.O. Box 8, Rensselaerville, N.Y. 12147

Bethlehem Historical Association, 1003 River Rd., 12158

Knox Historical Society, P.O. Box 11, Knox, N.Y. 12107

Westerlo Historical Society, 5912 State St., Westerlo, N.Y. 12193.

Janet Vine (Bethlehem).

Will Osterhout (Berne).

Albany County Historical Association (Wendy Burch), 9 Ten Broeck Place, Albany, N.Y. 12210.

Top, left: The original Vincent's Store, on the right, was located at the corner of Route 1 and West Woodstock Road in South Berne. The small hamlet was also known as Centerville prior to 1825, and has also been referred to as Mud Hollow.

Top, middle: Originally built by Oscar Taylor in 1844, Franklin Shultes and Arthur Adams moved their store to this location in 1898 from the Daniel Simmons Hotel in the hamlet of Berne.

Top, right: St. Paul's Lutheran Church was built in 1835, just west of the hamlet of Berne, and is still in use today. In January of 1845, it was the site of the first New York State Anti-Rent Convention.

Below (from left to right): left: Alice Begley, Town of Guilderland historian; Kevin Franklin, Town of Colonie historian; and Susan Leath, Town of Bethlehem historian.

Passengers on the Hudson, waiting
to enter Canal at Twenty-third
Street, 1870s.

SHARING THE HERITAGE

Historic profiles of businesses, organizations,

and families that have contributed to the

development and economic base of Albany

Albany Steel Inc. 38
Abele Tractor & Equipment Co., Inc. 42
Albany Pump Station 45
Albany County Historical Association 46
Security Supply Corporation 47

ALBANY STEEL INC.

In the very early 1900s, F. Arthur Hunsdorfer worked as regional sales manager for Carnegie Steel Corp. Hunsdorfer was responsible for covering all of upstate New York from Newburgh to the Canadian border on both sides of the Hudson River. Due to the lack of bridges across the Hudson at the time, Hunsdorfer usually only made sales calls on the eastern side of the river in the winter when he could drive across the ice. He put the car in neutral and placed a weight on the accelerator to hold it down. Then, exiting the vehicle, he stood on the running board outside the car, reached in and jammed the shifting lever into gear. The car

would start its slow progress across the river with Hunsdorfer ready to jump off at the first sign that the ice was cracking. He had a few close calls but never got wet.

It may have been this early experience that made him decide to start his own business; building a warehouse in one place and let most of his customers come to him.

In 1922, Hunsdorfer joined forces with two of his business associates, Ben Gifford, president of Gifford-Wood Company of Hudson and Walter Strope, purchasing agent for McKinney Steel of Albany. Gifford provided funding; Hunsdorfer and Strope were to run the business. The first business, named General Mill and Contractors' Supply Company was located in a vacant flower and vegetable stand at 899 Broadway, near the corner of Ferry Street, just north of today's Miss Albany Diner. It also had a small warehouse behind it that ran back to McGowan Street behind Broadway. Next door was the Boardman and Gray Piano Company.

After one year, Strope split and started a competing business, Strope Steel, on Terminal Street in Albany. Hunsdorfer, with Gifford's financial support, moved across the street to much larger quarters at 892 Broadway (now called 900 Broadway, housing Universal Auto Parts) and incorporated the new company as Albany Steel and Iron Supply Company.

The main product of Albany Steel and Iron Supply Company in 1922 was reinforcing bar. The city of Albany was slowly converting from cobblestone to concrete streets. Large blankets of steel reinforcing bars were fabricated to strengthen the concrete. Other products fabricated and warehoused by Albany Steel included hot and cold rolled steel bars, rolled bands and hoops (for making barrels), beams, angles, plate, sheet, tin plate and railroad track.

Since his new competitor, Strope, stored most of his inventory outside in an open yard, whenever a large rebar bid was requested, Hunsdorfer would drive up to Strope Steel on Terminal Street to see if Strope had enough inventory to bid the job. Hunsdorfer adjusted his bid accordingly.

In 1929, Albany Steel moved to new, much larger quarters at 45 Broadway, Menands. This location, currently Cransville Block, was located across the street from Albany's Hawkins Stadium, home of the Eastern Baseball League's Albany Senators. Each season Albany Steel could count on about a dozen broken windows from baseballs fouled straight back over the roof. Albany Steel always paid to repair the broken window but at least they got to keep the ball.

When this plant first opened, Hunsdorfer was worried that he had built it too far outside the city. Broadway was unpaved at the time and early photographs show a trolley track running along a dirt road flanked by weeds.

In the 1920s and 1930s, Albany Steel started to build one of the area's first trucking fleets to deliver steel. The stake trucks and flatbed trucks of the day were about the size of a pickup truck today. These trucks were used to deliver reinforcing bar and steel beams up to forty feet long. This was accomplished by running the beam up along the side of the truck and securing it to the side of the truck and front

bumper. It was not unusual to have beams running along both sides of the truck making it impossible to open either door; the driver climbed in through the window.

The 1920s were a time of great prosperity in the Albany area and the country as a whole and Albany Steel prospered and grew rapidly. The stock market crash and depression in 1929 and the 1930s slowed growth but Albany Steel was always prosperous. In the early 1940s,

the outbreak of war brought a large increase in government contracts, many originating through the Watervliet Arsenal. At the same time, steel shortages reached epidemic proportions. Albany Steel had more orders than they could fill. Steel Mills went into production twenty-four hours a day, seven days a week, trying to meet demand for raw material. Albany Steel's military contracts, including one to fabricate escape hatches to be mounted to the bottom of tanks, got priority over other work.

Albany Steel's expansion included the purchase of Hannibal Green's Sons of Troy. Hannibal Green had been originally formed in 1809, by Henry Nazro and Jacob Hart at 6 Lane's Row, east of River Street. The partnership ceased operations briefly during the War of 1812 because Nazro & Hart could not import iron hardware through the British blockade of the coast of New England. In 1820, their warehouse was completely gutted by the great fire in Downtown Troy but was rebuilt at 3 Lane's Row shortly thereafter. In the earliest days, Hannibal Green sold hardware, nails, iron bars, anvils, vices, Smith's bellows, mill saws, cutlery, horseshoe iron, and manufactured "steel springs of every description." They were also listed as distributors of Fairbanks Celebrated Scales.

Nazro & Hart (1809) became Nazro & Green (1834), Green & Cramer (1838), Hannibal Green (1852) and later, Hannibal Green's Sons (1875). In 1855, they moved from 231-233 River Street to the corner of Albany (later Broadway) and Fourth Street that at the time was called "the old Corning lot."

Ads from the 1870s listed Hannibal Green as "the importers and dealers in iron, steel, and heavy hardware, Agents for Burden's Iron, horseshoes and boiler rivets." An early 1800s, Troy newspaper said that Hannibal Green was "...the direct representative of the Burden Iron Company for its iron, a product which has a worldwide reputation." When Hannibal Green was purchased by Albany Steel, Hannibal Green was housed in one of the Burden Iron Buildings at the foot of Monroe Street.

Albany Steel expanded into the fabrication of structural steel for buildings and bridges through the purchase of the Claussen Iron Company on Tivoli Street in Albany. Claussen was comprised of three buildings and a large warehouse and structural yard on the south side of Tivoli Street, just west of Pearl Street. One of Albany's most historic and beautiful buildings, the D&H Building, now State University Plaza, was fabricated at Claussen Iron. The building was designed by Marcus T. Reynolds and construction started in 1916. Also part of this project was the fabrication of the adjacent *Albany Evening Journal* Building, thought by most people to be part of the D&H Building, but actually a separate building.

On July 10, 1976, Albany Steel officially moved into a newly constructed modern facility at 566 Broadway in Menands. This facility, approximately 240,000 square feet, sells steel, fabricated steel and machine parts.

Albany Steel's Service Center does warehousing and cutting of plate, sheet, bar, structural and specialty steel with the area's largest stacker crane system housing 10,000 tons of bar stock and several computer controlled torch cutting machines and state-of-the-art saws and plate shears. The Steel Fabrication Department can fabricate almost any steel structure. A computer-controlled drill line drills structural steel and plate. The Fabrication Department also does welding, shot blasting, and painting, as well as bending and rolling of plate, bar and sheet, and fabricating reinforcing bar and rebar cages. Albany Steel can also produce machine parts in its Machining Division.

In June 1985, Peter Hess, former vice president and general manager of Albany Steel, bought the company from Richard Hunsdorfer,

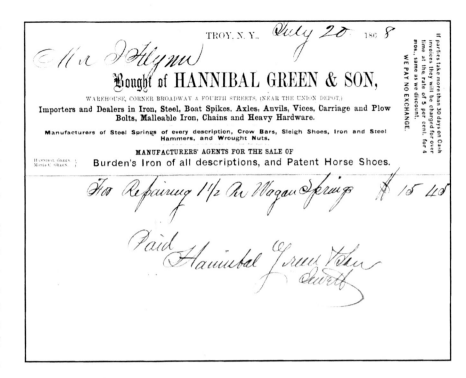

who retired. Current managers include: President Peter J. Hess; Sales Manager Benjamin J. Van Duzer; Plant Manager Brian Keefe; Machining Manager Joe Westervelt; Controller Kimberly O'Rourke; Credit Manager Deanna Mantica and Fabrication Manager Max Meyer.

Today Albany Steel is Albany's largest and oldest Steel Service Center. Their history goes back 200 years to 1809. They have survived major fires, the War of 1812, the Civil War, two World Wars, major depressions, five major strikes, and many periods of iron and steel shortages and rationing. As the elder Hunsdorfer demonstrated by crossing the river on the ice, the ability to survive lies in ability to adapt to constant challenges.

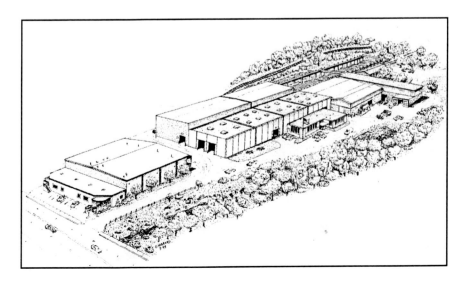

ABELE TRACTOR & EQUIPMENT CO., INC.

Abele Tractor & Equipment Company, Inc. is a 140 year old company. It is currently in its fifth generation of family ownership and operation. Its core business is sales, renting/leasing and servicing of construction equipment. The company also sells and services equipment for grounds maintenance for both commercial and consumer type customers. Abele Tractor is the dealer for fifty plus major manufacturers of equipment.

The company traces its roots back to the 1870s when German emigrant Nickolas Miller opened a blacksmith shop a mile north of the livestock yards at West Albany on Everett Road. He had eight children, four sons and four daughters. The youngest of the sons, William, served as an apprentice at the New York Central Railroad shops situated nearby. Eventually, with his two brothers John and Frank, they opened their own business at the same location as their father. John ran a blacksmith shop, Frank opened a wheelwright shop, and William ran the machine shop. The fourth son, Charles,

❖

Above: William Miller June 10, 1904, as seen at the tiller of the car he hand built in his machine shop on Everett Road. It was among the first automobiles to be seen in the Albany Area.

Below: Ken and his wife Thelma with their two sons, Rod and Warren Abele, c. 1975.

was a judge who sometimes held court on the second floor of William's machine shop. The brothers were an entrepreneurial and ambitious family, and had an impact on the Albany area more then they could have possibly envisioned.

The community recognized William for his exceptional skills as a machinist. He built one of the first steam-powered cars in the Albany area. In the early days of West Albany's fire department, he built the first two pieces of fire apparatus that the company used.

William, and his wife Emma, had a daughter, Thelma, who would play a key factor in what would be a major transition of the company during the twentieth century. In December of 1940 she married Kenneth Abele from New Rochelle, New York. Kenneth was hired by William as an apprentice in 1940, and would become part of the third generation of the business started by Thelma's grandfather.

In 1943, William retired, and Ken and Thelma took over business operations. During WWII the company had a priority rating issued by the government to buy structural steel and fuel. This made the company one of the few places in Albany that could meet the demands for repairs and maintenance of equipment because, at the time, new machinery was virtually impossible to obtain.

After the war the nature of the business changed from predominately repairing to selling and servicing construction and consumer outdoor power equipment. More land was acquired, new buildings built, and in 1959, the business incorporated as Abele Tractor & Equipment Co., Inc. Ken and Thelma set the precedents for the company, hiring a staff of knowledgeable mechanics and working with private and state contractors. This set the stage that would see Abele taking part in the development of the major state building projects in the Albany area in the 1960-1970s, including the state university, state office campus complex, Empire State Plaza, the network of arterial highways that surround the city and the New York State Thruway. Abele was one of the first companies to start the business of renting and leasing construction equipment.

By the 1970s, having grown the company and increasing the work force, the Abeles were making a major impact in the area. One

past employee said that Ken and Thelma were "all business and they strived for perfection, encouraging those around them to do so as well." The company had grown from a machine shop, and was then positioned to become a part of the major heavy construction equipment business.

Ken and Thelma had two sons, Warren and Rod, who became the fourth generation of the family business. By the 1970-1980s they became an integral part of the business and its development. Ken and Thelma retired in 1983, and leadership was put in the hands of their sons.

During the 1980s, the company began increasing its industrial product lines of earthmoving, material handling and demolition equipment. During this time to present there has been a tenfold increase to the point where the company now conducts business internationally.

Under their leadership, the company saw increases in staff, employing several mechanics in servicing large and small construction equipment. Many come from various backgrounds, and in the words of one employee; "You're more than a number here, the Abeles want you to be part of the family."

❖

Above: One of Abele's equipment yards, 2012.

Below: Left to right, Jeff and Rod Abele, 2012.

As in its past, Abele has been there for its community in times of crisis and need. Often the company is one of the first responders to disasters in the northeast and was there following the September 11 attacks in 2001. Abele has also played major roles at various times of flooding of the Hudson and Mohawk Rivers, and surrounding areas including the flooding caused by Hurricane Irene in 2011.

Presently, the company is seeing its fifth generation of family entrepreneurship. In the late 1980s, the company employed Jeff Abele the son of Rod and Sharon Abele. As a team, Warren, Rod and Jeff have continued to grow and diversify Abele's equipment fleet. It has seen expansion in property both at its original location on Everett Road and further south at the Port of Albany. Abele Tractor is moving into the future with sales throughout the United States and many foreign countries.

Abele's mission statement is, "to be committed to making sure that every customer is treated like our only customer." With this in mind the company is in a position to continue business in the twenty-first century.

C. H. Evans Brewing Company at the Albany Pump Station is Albany's premier location for delicious food and award-winning hand crafted beer. With up to ten in-house brews to choose from, the Pump Station is sure to have something for every beer lover. It is a unique venue with a friendly atmosphere that will make your visit a memorable one. The space is simply amazing.

There are actually two histories at the Albany Pump Station. The first is the building itself which was constructed in 1874 to house two steam powered water pumping engines. These engines supplied domestic water for the residents of Albany. The building was expanded in 1895 and three more pumps were added. In 1927 the Pump Station moved over 7 billion gallons of water up to the Bleecker Reservoir, which is now Bleecker Stadium.

Two massive overhead bridge-cranes were used to service the engines. These 105 year old cranes remain today and are still functional. In 1932 the Alcove Reservoir was put into service and the Pump Station ceased operation. In 1974 the building was placed on the National Historic Register.

The other history comes from the Evans family. They were in the commercial brewing business for three generations. The original brewery was built in Hudson, New York in 1786. It continued production until prohibition in 1920. At the turn of the century (1900) the brewery produced over 69,000 barrels of beer, which was distributed throughout the Northeast.

Neil Evans revives this rich heritage here at the Albany Pump Station. Surviving C. H. Evans Brewing Company memorabilia is displayed in the establishment, which opened in 1999, as well as pictures of the Pump Station as it appeared at the turn of the century. Dramatic forty foot ceilings and an industrial look showcase the award winning brewery which is

located in the middle of the restaurant. An open display kitchen highlights the wide ranging menu with options for all tastes.

ALBANY COUNTY HISTORICAL ASSOCIATION

❖

Above: Archeology Camp, Summer, 2009.

Below: Ten Broeck Mansion interior, 2008.

The Albany County Historical Association (ACHA) was founded in 1945. It is a private, not-for-profit educational corporation, having a permanent charter from the NYS Board of Regents (the University of the State of New York). It is governed by a twenty-nine member Board of Trustees and operates according to its Constitution and By-laws. Its headquarters is located at the historic Ten Broeck Mansion in the Arbor Hill neighborhood of the city of Albany, New York. The mission of the ACHA is to preserve, present, and promote the rich history and culture of Albany County.

The ACHA is committed to educational and cultural outreach. It accomplishes this through exhibits, lectures, concerts, tours, and other educational activities. These include a Living History Day in May and a summer Archeology Camp for children. History comes alive during Living History Day, which includes historic re-enactors, hands-on educational displays, and tours of the historic Ten Broeck Mansion, all free to the public. The week-long Archeology Camp in July is open to children entering fifth and sixth grade. Scholarships are available for those neighborhood students unable to afford the fee.

One of the ACHA's most important responsibilities is to preserve and maintain the historic Ten Broeck Mansion and its Collections. Revolutionary War Brigadier General (and Albany Mayor) Abraham Ten Broeck built the mansion in 1798 and it has played a significant role in Albany County's history over the last 200 years.

The ACHA is a vital anchor to the Arbor Hill community. As such, the organization is involved in the promotion of the neighborhood, serves on several committees including the Arbor Hill Implementation Team, which is overseeing city plans for improvements to the Arbor Hill area, as well as its subcommittees focused on business development in the area and as a redevelopment tool, the promotion of local arts and culture in the immediate neighborhood.

The ACHA actively partners with other historical and cultural institutions, and works to promote Albany County's rich history with events held at the Ten Broeck Mansion as well as other locations around the Capital District.

In 1923, at the age of twenty-two, William M. Bennett moved to Selkirk, New York and established a plumbing contractor business in the hamlet at 198 Maple Avenue. In 1926, Harold L. Williams, Sr., joined Bennett in business. Williams relocated from Laurens, New York bringing his extensive knowledge of the plumbing industry with him to Selkirk. In 1929, Earl D. Vadney joined the business as bookkeeper.

The plumbing contractor business developed, creating the need for additional warehousing. In 1931 a new facility was erected at 196 Maple Avenue. Having undergone several additions, this building is now the current corporate headquarters for Security Supply Corporation.

In 1933 the country was in a state of economic despair and severe depression. The three business partners had the foresight to turn these circumstances into opportunity. In those challenging economic times, manufacturers were looking for companies to help sell their product. These men put their plumbing tool belts down and became a wholesale supply house for plumbing products. In 1934, Bennett, Williams and Vadney officially formed Security Supply Corporation.

Late in 1934, they began the process of expanding the company in New York by opening a branch in Albany. The Schenectady branch was soon launched in 1938. From 1942 to 1945, during World War II, all locations were closed while the three gentlemen served their country. Bennett served in the Navy, Vadney served in the Army and Williams served with the Schenectady-based prime defense contractor, General Electric. Following the war, all locations were reopened as material became available for sale. Security Supply grew and prospered during the 1940s, 1950s, and 1960s.

After many years of dedicated service to the company, Bennett retired in 1961, Vadney suddenly and tragically passed away in 1962 and Williams retired in 1966. The second generation was ready and prepared to step in and carry on the legacy of Security Supply, as they had become part of the operation as it grew. This generation resumed the process of expansion with the addition of several branches. They opened a branch in Glens Falls in 1968, Johnstown in 1982 and Plattsburgh in 1986. They extended their services to Western Massachusetts by opening the North Adams branch in 1989. Heading further north in New York, Security Supply purchased Hyde Plumbing Supply in 1994, which consisted of stores in Watertown, Massena and Ogdensbury. The Ogdensburg branch closed in 1996. The expansion continued through Downstate New York with the opening of the Kingston branch in 1998 and quickly extended to Poughkeepsie with the purchase of Dutchess Wholesale in 2003. The Saratoga Springs branch was established with the purchase of National Supply in 2004, and the Massena branch merged with Plattsburgh in 2006, brining the total locations to twelve.

Security Supply Corporation is a full line supply house, carrying an extensive line of plumbing, heating, air conditioning, water pump and treatment products, pipe, valves and fittings. The company is diversified in the markets served, selling to the repair/remodeling contractor, new home construction market, commercial construction, fuel oil dealers, HVAC contractors, schools, colleges and public facilities. Services also extend to homeowners with the newly renovated Bath Expressions Showrooms by Security Supply. These showrooms are located at the Albany, Schenectady, Glen Falls, Saratoga Springs and Poughkeepsie branch locations.

For more information about the following publications or about publishing your own book, please call
Historical Publishing Network at 800-749-9790 or visit www.lammertinc.com.

Albemarle & Charlottesville:
An Illustrated History of the First 150 Years
Black Gold: The Story of Texas Oil & Gas
Garland: A Contemporary History
Historic Abilene: An Illustrated History
Historic Alamance County: An Illustrated History
Historic Albuquerque: An Illustrated History
Historic Alexandria: An Illustrated History
Historic Amarillo: An Illustrated History
Historic Anchorage: An Illustrated History
Historic Austin: An Illustrated History
Historic Baldwin County: A Bicentennial History
Historic Baton Rouge: An Illustrated History
Historic Beaufort County: An Illustrated History
Historic Beaumont: An Illustrated History
Historic Bexar County: An Illustrated History
Historic Birmingham: An Illustrated History
Historic Brazoria County: An Illustrated History
Historic Brownsville: An Illustrated History
Historic Charlotte:
An Illustrated History of Charlotte and Mecklenburg County
Historic Chautauqua County: An Illustrated History
Historic Cheyenne: A History of the Magic City
Historic Clayton County: An Illustrated History
Historic Comal County: An Illustrated History
Historic Corpus Christi: An Illustrated History
Historic DeKalb County: An Illustrated History
Historic Denton County: An Illustrated History
Historic Edmond: An Illustrated History
Historic El Paso: An Illustrated History
Historic Erie County: An Illustrated History
Historic Fayette County: An Illustrated History
Historic Fairbanks: An Illustrated History
Historic Gainesville & Hall County: An Illustrated History
Historic Gregg County: An Illustrated History
Historic Hampton Roads: Where America Began
Historic Hancock County: An Illustrated History
Historic Henry County: An Illustrated History
Historic Hood County: An Illustrated History
Historic Houston: An Illustrated History
Historic Hunt County: An Illustrated History
Historic Illinois: An Illustrated History
Historic Kern County:
An Illustrated History of Bakersfield and Kern County
Historic Lafayette:
An Illustrated History of Lafayette & Lafayette Parish
Historic Laredo:
An Illustrated History of Laredo & Webb County
Historic Lee County: The Story of Fort Myers & Lee County
Historic Louisiana: An Illustrated History
Historic Mansfield: A Bicentennial History
Historic Midland: An Illustrated History
Historic Mobile:
An Illustrated History of the Mobile Bay Region

Historic Montgomery County:
An Illustrated History of Montgomery County, Texas
Historic Ocala: The Story of Ocala & Marion County
Historic Oklahoma: An Illustrated History
Historic Oklahoma County: An Illustrated History
Historic Omaha:
An Illustrated History of Omaha and Douglas County
Historic Orange County: An Illustrated History
Historic Osceola County: An Illustrated History
Historic Ouachita Parish: An Illustrated History
Historic Paris and Lamar County: An Illustrated History
Historic Pasadena: An Illustrated History
Historic Passaic County: An Illustrated History
Historic Pennsylvania An Illustrated History
Historic Philadelphia: An Illustrated History
Historic Prescott:
An Illustrated History of Prescott & Yavapai County
Historic Richardson: An Illustrated History
Historic Rio Grande Valley: An Illustrated History
Historic Rogers County: An Illustrated History
Historic San Marcos: An Illustrated History
Historic Santa Barbara: An Illustrated History
Historic Scottsdale: A Life from the Land
Historic Shelby County: An Illustrated History
Historic Shreveport-Bossier:
An Illustrated History of Shreveport & Bossier City
Historic South Carolina: An Illustrated History
Historic Smith County: An Illustrated History
Historic Temple: An Illustrated History
Historic Texarkana: An Illustrated History
Historic Texas: An Illustrated History
Historic Victoria: An Illustrated History
Historic Tulsa: An Illustrated History
Historic Wake County: An Illustrated History
Historic Warren County: An Illustrated History
Historic Williamson County: An Illustrated History
Historic Wilmington & The Lower Cape Fear:
An Illustrated History
Historic York County: An Illustrated History
Iron, Wood & Water: An Illustrated History of Lake Oswego
Jefferson Parish: Rich Heritage, Promising Future
Miami's Historic Neighborhoods: A History of Community
Old Orange County Courthouse: A Centennial History
Plano: An Illustrated Chronicle
The New Frontier:
A Contemporary History of Fort Worth & Tarrant County
Rich With Opportunity: Images of Beaumont and Jefferson County
San Antonio, City Exceptional
The San Gabriel Valley: A 21st Century Portrait
Southwest Louisiana: A Treasure Revealed
The Spirit of Collin County
Valley Places, Valley Faces
Water, Rails & Oil: Historic Mid & South Jefferson County